Table of Contents

Morning Light 1
The Forest.. 2
The Journey 3
My Heart 4
Abandoned 5
The Farm 6
The Guest 7
Free Fall 8
Workman at the Chapel Door..................................... 9
On the Wing... 10
Pilgrim Place 11
Retreat Life 12
Sacred Space 13
Today.. 14
A Walk 15
Timeless 16
Etched... 17

Mornings	18
The Lighthouse	19
Climb	20
Beauty	21
Dawn	22
Noticed	23
Hunter Eagle	24
Bear Cub	25
Wolf and I	26
Water Song	27
Mother's Cookbook	29
Father's Oak Trees	30
Turtle Dove	31
Robin	32
Peace	33
Sometimes	34
Blue	35
A Time Long Ago	36
Beyond Time	37
Inside the Window	38
Ode to an Anna's Hummingbird	39
Autumn of Life	41
Yearning	42
Night	43
Doors	44
Wonder	45

Waiting for the Light

Poetic Reflections

JANET FISHER

Waiting for the Light
Copyright © 2023 by Janet Fisher

All rights reserved. No part of this publication
may be reproduced, distributed, or transmitted
in any form or by any means, including
photocopying, recording, or other electronic
or mechanical methods, without the prior
written permission of the author, except in the
case of brief quotations embodied in critical
reviews and certain other non-commercial
uses permitted by copyright law.

Tellwell Talent
www.tellwell.ca

ISBN
978-0-2288-5064-9 (Paperback)
978-0-2288-5065-6 (eBook)

Deep Places	46
The Giants	47
Years	48
Like a Sparrow	49
Finding My Way	50
Home	51
Fear	53
Ode to a Turtle Dove	54
Listen	55
Grandmother	56
Thirst	57
Desert	58
Cathedral Grove	59
The Sky	60
Witnessed	61
Pandemic Recovery	63
Shadows	64
Memories We Keep	65
Homecoming	66
The Night Owl	67
Pulse	68
Great Spirit	69
Resting	70
Navigate	71
Tranquility	72
Melancholy	73

The Mirror of Time	74
Arbutus Tree	75
Lone Tree	76
Joshua Tree	77
Sunflower	78
A Summer Morning	79
Lullaby	80
Wee Folk	81
Tiger Lily	82
Rain on Glass	83
The Gardener	84
On Growing Older	85
A Gentle Man	86
Trapped	87
Watching	89
My Years	90
Sunshine and Water	91

Introduction

"And for all this, nature is never spent;
There lives the dearest freshness deep down things."

~ Gerard Manley Hopkins

I believe this to be true. I know this to be true, deep down in my being. And so, informed by "deep down things" such as the vibrance of the natural world and the complexity of human nature, I began my writing journey. I write because I can find no better forge and anvil to hammer out the longings of my heart and to describe the awe-inspiring beauty of nature.

Much of my writing features forests, oceans, mountains and light. Nature has always informed and inspired my writing - a walk in the woods, my husband's roses, a lone tree, an ocean swell. Then there is human nature, the joys and challenges of life, the laughter, and the tears. This is my story too.

My writing emerges out of an ongoing sense of wonder as I engage life with my senses and spirit. Robert Frost said that "A poem begins with a lump in the throat." I would add, that, to me, a poem also begins as a bridge into another world, a portal into imagination where trees and animals come alive, and people are authentic, vulnerable and true. My intent for you, the reader, is that my words may offer you a sense of wonder, belonging and healing amidst all of life's challenges.

At the start of my writing journey, the poetry forms I chose ranged from formal verse (i.e., iambic pentameter, haiku, rhyming couplets) to free verse and prose. As my writing journey matured, I became more contemplative and enigmatic in my forms. This has freed me to explore emotional nuances in a more contemplative way.

My experience as a host at Rivendell Retreat Centre on Bowen Island, B.C., has taught me to seek sacred space, to leave room for personal growth and to experience the depths of the human spirit. I have observed so much courage and tenacity in the stories of our retreatants!

I am thankful to my family and Instagram friends who have encouraged me. A special thank you to my husband and best friend, Gerry, who has supported me all the way.

September 2023

Morning Light

In this morning's dawn
across a dew-green lawn
a turtledove called to me
from a shady-leafed tree.

And I, sleepy and slow,
replied in morning's soft glow
to this one I could not see
waiting for the light with me.

In that moment we shared
a holy silence prepared
for a day fresh and new,
a communion of two.

The Forest

The forest slows my hurried pace,
revealing treasures only found
where faeries tread, but leave no trace
on verdant leaves, or needled ground.

I walk these woods in reverie
seeking all treasures I might find
and such a trove of gems I see,
I pause to hold them in my mind.

Red huckleberries, tart yet sweet,
and grasses dancing in the breeze,
songbirds in deeper groves, who greet
the morning mist rise through the trees.

I taste the freshness of this place.
I see the ferns bow down in awe
I hear the sounds of sacred space
and then, reluctantly, withdraw.

The Journey

Sometimes
a person
comes along my
path's bend
who travels with
darkness;
so in her
soul sadness,
I want to heart mend;
the hardest world
to mend
is the one within
the heart,
like the dry desert,
it is a wild, fierce place,
words unspoken,
grief unsaid.

And so I asked
to be her friend.

My Heart

My heart belongs
to the sea;
Her siren call to me
chants from above
a lilting song of love
and resounds from below
where the ancient
currents flow;
She is a moody lover,
sometimes a fitful mother,
capricious, wild and free,
but forever She will be
my beacon of eternity,

Her waves lick hungrily
against a salty shore
drumming an ancient rhythm,
an eternal haunting hymn
drawing my thirsty soul
into the depths of wonder.

Eternity at my door.

Abandoned

One time I found
an old abandoned ship,
grey and worn
by wind and weather
and torn down strip by strip.
And once an eagle feather
caught my eye
in stormy weather,
clinging to the ground
under a low grey sky.
And then a moonstone,
smoothed and round,
polished by longer weather,
as I was passing by.

Such hidden treasures when
I simply look around;
how much more, then
in a sister or a brother,
grey and worn by inner weather,
and longing to be found.

The Farm

There's a story here
of a bygone day
when boots were muddied
and packed with clay
as people struggled
to make the earth pay,
of lives transplanted
from far away,
of unending labour
and times of play,
silent prayers calling
for help from above,
hope for tomorrow,
nurtured in love.

It's also my story.
I'm transplanted too.

The Guest

He would not talk at all
and sat in silence by the door;
his face was solemn with a pall,
the pain still eating at his core.

And so we brought him to our farm.

Poland was his ancestral place;
his true home was his family,
torn from him in the cruel face
of war, despite their hopeless plea.

Mother would place me on his lap
to see if I could comfort him
I'd feel his arms around me wrap,
as if I could somehow set him free.

Never to see his home again;
never to feel a loved one's arm
his leg lost, as so many men
broken and feeling wartime's harm.

And so we brought him to our farm.

Free Fall

What do I know
of myself?
Is there an inner me,
a tangled twine ball
longing to free fall,
clambering to call out
as a child might
in a game of hide and seek:
"Here I am, find me?"

The greater, grander plans
of life escape me;
how to release,
take my hands off the wheel,
watch them swim away
in this crazy stream
of life;
something of me
hears heart laughter;

something of me
is hidden inside
these words.

Workman at the Chapel Door

He stands
at the door
watching the Brothers
singing the psalms
of the sages.
Boots worn,
heart torn,
forlorn,
he struggles to turn
the pages.

Yet in those
weathered eyes
are etched
the anthems
of the ages.

Janet Fisher

On the Wing

I watched an eagle on the wing,
riding the wind and soaring free,
majestically, like a king
rising above humanity.

And then a tiny songbird rose
above the bushes, to the sky,
adorned in showy, brighter clothes,
singing as she caught my eye.

How hardy and yet wise are they
who rise upon their wings to where
sky opens into brighter day,
above the worries and the care

Pilgrim Place

The desert is my pilgrim place
when my soul is worn and weary,
and searching for a sacred space
where I can glimpse eternity.
I see the high blue firmament
arching over this sandy plain
as I search for life discernment,
so then to find myself again.
But most of all I come to find
time to pause, to
listen and to hear
that still small voice
inside my mind, speaking to my
listening ear.

Retreat Life

Birthed as a dream
of respite for the weary,
a living stream
of ordinary people
pass through this place,
seeking sacred space.

And other ordinary people
hold the doors open wide
to welcome inside
the wounded,
who need to reside
in a spacious place
where they can embrace
themselves - loved and beloved,
so that hope may rebirth
like the greening earth.

Sacred Space

There is Deep Magic dwelling here
as love and light shine strong and deep,
with goblets raised to bring good cheer,
our hearts then turn to deeper sleep.

While pilgrims call this sacred space
In Rivendell's beguiling green,
the Celtics say, "Tis a thin place"
where lives the lore of things unseen.

Such Magic - how can one explain:
birdsong echoing through the trees,
then - deeper musical refrain
of canticles on bended knees.

Today

Today
I wandered
in the forest
gleaning the fallen
and broken branches,
holding them close
to my beating heart,

hallowed

and I found there
in the silence,
a serenity within me
as I remembered other
fallen and broken things

hallowed.

A Walk

I walked amongst the trees today,
feeling rather melancholy,
hoping they'd have something to say,
but they had not a word for me.

So I turned then, to the roses.
Thoughtfully, they spoke to me
of how the bloom opens, closes,
until at last, it is fully free.

Now I know how the wild rosebush
has understood her destiny,
and I am waiting for the lush
opening of the bloom in me.

Timeless

The morning air is near still
pregnant with dew light;
there is mystery
in the unknowing
of this new day
where I can be,
just simply be,
in the silence.

Yet this solitude
of sadness lingers,
an open question
in a sea of questions
and the timeless
aches of humanity;
my soul cries out
but there are no answers
except for the slow ticking of time;

perhaps tomorrow will bring
good news.

Etched

Tiny tendrils
reaching for light
and pansies
kneeling low
are etched
upon my sight.

A feast of bright.

How lovely
to be so graced
by small things,
white and blue.
And so, I wonder:

Is this you,
disguised
in morning hue?

Mornings

Some mornings
I rise slowly
in the dim light
wondering
if this is the
beginning
of senescence;
bones creaking,
head aching,
I struggle to
awaken;

but then comes
a resurgence of
energy
as I sense
a bright
Renaissance
rising.

The Lighthouse

She leans listless
on the cliff face;
seaward she leans,
worn and weathered
by the slow ticking of time
and the years
of savage seas
and wayward winds;
no steady hands remain
to set the light now;
the sounds of the
Light Keeper's children
in carefree play
have drifted away.

Listen now,
to the hollow keening
of a lonely lighthouse.

Climb

I would like
to climb high,
very high,
above my city,
above my world,
a steep climb
above time.

Perhaps then,
gazing down
upon this place
I've called home,
I would see the face
of God,
yearning
over this turning,
darkening dome.

Beauty

I went looking for beauty but beauty found me,
when I opened my eyes to see:
a high flying kite so wild and free,
the rising swell of an ancient sea,
an old ship moored by a village quay,
an eagle in flight to high aerie,
a west mountain's lofty majesty,
the frosted edge of a winter tree,
a child singing out in joyous glee,
a whispered prayer on bended knee,
the hopeful eyes of a refugee.

I went looking for beauty but beauty found me,
when I opened my eyes to see.

Dawn

Damp and dreary dawned the day
which lingered lazily in the east;
the herald of dawn, in lonely tone
echoed his first, faint greeting.

Then like a ghost, the storm arose,
tearing trees asunder.
The earth was shaken as forked fingers
probed across the sky and
creatures whimpered pleas of mercy.
And then it was gone, leaving a wasteland
limp from wrath.

Are memories of violence
as quickly gone as this;
does mercy reign
and peace on earth
or are we still in labour,
waiting for that final day
when we will have rebirth?

Noticed

As others
passed by,
you noticed me,
looking deep
within my being,
seeing the sadness
that sometimes
lingers there,
and also
the small joys;
my soul
made a small
leap of hope;

because
you noticed me
as others passed by.

Hunter Eagle

She poses proudly
surveying her domain,
looking disdainfully
around the fertile plain
as if not aware
of creatures hiding there.

A pause, a swoop,
a quick dive down;
she makes the loop,
then gathers up her gown
to wait again.

Bear Cub

Little bear cub,
hobbling behind
your mama,
you have no voice yet,
deep and growly
and true,
so you must let
her speak for you.

Sometimes my voice
is muted too,
silenced by grief or fear.
So then,
I too must trust
a parent
who is always
near.

Wolf and I

His
golden eyes
held mine
and
drew me
into
the wild.
I could not
pass by
this loner,
leader spy
or even say
goodbye.

and so
I lingered there
inside his stare
my heart
laid bare.

Water Song

Listening
to the sound of water
tumbling over stones
stills my soul.
My breathing slows
as the melody
flows over me,
Nature's lullaby
cradling me.

And then the stones
begin to speak,
"Listen.
this is the music
of the spheres
singing
your soul story.

You belong.
you are loved
and you are
not alone
in this perilous
yet sacred
Universe."

Mother's Cookbook

Mother's cookbook
was covered with flour, butter,
molasses and laughter.
Leaves were pressed into
the corners of a page
and tea stains were everywhere.
Sometimes she wrote "haha"
on the page or "think".
I never did coax out from her
her recipe for brown bread.
She loved much and laughed often
but was frugal with her praise.
That was reserved for school grades
or the Golden Rule

but her memories
were rich and powerful
as she turned the pages
of her one hundred year old life.

Father's Oak Trees

Father planted
oak trees around our old house,
life forces to last longer than his own.
He appointed them to watch over us
in the same way he did.
They sent out roots, reaching
tough tentacles into the soft soil.
Acorns drifted downward
in a shower of wood shavings and sparkles.
There was safety in these sages
who kept watch over our home,
sentinels tall and strong.
The wisdom of these giants surrounded me
while the ancient voices of the forest spoke,

"We are your friends; do not be troubled;
we have been here for generations,
offering shade and strength and comfort.
Enter into our silence.
Listen to the wisdom of the ages.

Be still."

Turtle Dove

As hands that touch within a glove,
as murmurs from a turtle dove,
as lone petitions in the night;
so darkness is infused with light.

As chimes that ring out from above,
as moonbeams reflect divine love,
as hummingbirds in spritely flight;
so darkness is infused with light.

Robin

Robin on the treetop,
are you singing to me
or are you singing a melody
of dry feathered nests,
and sky-blue eggs,
fat worms from the earth,
and water-splashed legs?

A red breasted chorus of mirth.

Peace

Peace lives within,
like a sleeping child.
She is your dearest kin
when fear is running wild.
You cannot always find her
yet she seeks you in the storm,
and brings you healing myrrh,
to soothe your aching form.

And this one gift will she bestow:
She will help you to surrender
her enemy, your foe:
that tiger in your centre
which will not let you go.

Sometimes

Sometimes my memory wanders away
to another time and a distant day
when children ran freely
through fields and sun
and nobody worried about our fun
and we knew the names of everyone.
When grandparents mattered
and had their say
about chores and reading before our play.

Two rivers ran through our little town
where we would swim and laugh, and clown
from daylight to twilight with joyous delight.
Over the hills and vales we'd roam
until the train whistle called us home.

I write this now with a smile and a sigh
knowing I never shall bid goodbye
to a memory so clear and bold
that it can never, ever grow old.

Blue

When all of life seems
dim and blue,
but grass is green
and blessed with dew
and time stands still,
the light shines through;
feasting on this epiphany
I wonder what living
is meant to be,
only this
blinding blue mystery?
Or is the light
shining inside so near
that night will disappear?
Where from such light
I hardly know, but this I do;

It shines for me.
It shines for you.

A Time Long Ago

In a time long ago
when the days were slow
and new beginnings
had eons to grow,
I measured the future
in far away stars
where dreams were
flung out like diamonds
into brightening skies
with a never ending glow.

But now my reminiscing
on those beginnings
has given me clearer sight
and those far away stars
have drawn nearer,
into a longer and deeper night,
infused with a brighter
and never ending Light.

Beyond Time

As I turn the pages of my life,
I come across a memory once lived
and still cherished:
beyond time, I see a little girl
finding adventure in branches and trees,
the kind you climb and explore;
branches that swing with the breeze
and with a little girl's weight
dangling upside down,
tangled hair flying, unbridled glee:
and then -
to watch and wait, until
through those branches,
she would see a Narnia world
where trees could talk and even walk
and friends were faithful, brave and free.

What a pleasure it would be,
if, through poetry,
with Narnia eyes, we'd see.

Janet Fisher

Inside the Window

I looked inside
the window of my heart
and opened up this whisper:

Creator of all,
hear my plea,
my long desire;
give clear eyes
to loved ones dear,
illumine our way,
stay near
and grant
that we may turn
and follow on
with hearts that yearn
as we walk this life
together.

Ode to an Anna's Hummingbird

Oh, bird of flight, so quick and bright,
how shall I catch you in my sight?
So small and yet ferocious too,
you bring such energy with you,
rising upon your jetted air.
My eyes are searching everywhere.

Ah! Now I see you rising up
above the nectar in the cup,
a flash of green and brightest red,
away from harm you spritely fled.
I do not blame your quick escape;
I simply watch with eyes agape.

So would I be as deft as you,
to fly the world and escape too,
this life which sometimes can be dull.
To shining places I would scull;
upon the wings of words I'd flee
away - to drink sweet poetry.

Thus you and I, though small in size,
would helicopter in the skies.
To wider worlds we then could glide,
where sweetest nectar does reside,
till, satiated, then return
to rest until, again, we yearn.

Autumn of Life

These rows of flaming autumn trees,
marching on in the gentle breeze
are calling me to march on too,
for I have still much life to do;
heart words to write;
and thus to share
my inner thoughts,
like breathing prayer.
So on through life
and loss and pain
I shall then learn to live again.

Autumn brings a slower calm
much like a thoughtful, quiet psalm
or one last rose's fragrant balm.
Timeless and elegant,
triumphant and sad,
Love's beguilement
musically clad.

Yearning

As leaves begin to turn,
I begin to yearn
for those warm summer days;
flowers in their prime,
that still, quiet time
when the world was so ablaze
in green and azure blue
and the wild birds flew
in the sun's bright rays.

Still,
as I wander these cooler fall days,
I gain a wiser gaze
in the altar of my heart;
my heart, growing warmer
sings a song of praise
for this intoxicating air
so crisp and rare.
Earth's once more ablaze
with dazzling displays.
Trees, crimson red and fair.
fling a final flare.

Autumn's fiery prayer.

Night

When the night is long
and the heart is weary,
the light fades in;
I rise slow to
another day
of fractured light
and turn again
to a new day of
beginning bright.

The morning murmurs
with luminous light,
branches reaching high
on a soft pastel sky
and breezes wafting gently
as if to say goodbye
to Winter's stay and
hello to a warming earth,
celebrating
Spring's rebirth.

Doors

Closed doors,
cracked and old
hold in the dark
where there are no answers;
who will come and bring
a shaft of light?
Yet watch and wait
for when the night is darkest
there is a dew dawn breaking;
my soul quest
is to live inside this Mystery,
to see the deeper
streams of life;
so I will continue then to seek
and with my muse to speak;
as long as life will
offer time
enough for me
to so untwine
this Mystery of life
I'll seek a brave
and bright new earth.

Wonder

I will sing a song
of wonder;
I will hear the story
inside each woman
and cradle each life,
to honor
the joy of friendships,
the hunger of souls,
the curiosity of minds
and
the wisdom of suffering,
to awaken the good news
that the King of all kings
stoops down to wash our feet
and looking up
into our faces says,

"I understand."

Deep Places

May
the deep places
within you
leap up and shout
for joy;
may the dark days
be few,
may love
become
your signature;
may all your
adventures
become fresh
and new
and may the
sea
of your longing
come home to
rest.

The Giants

The silence of the giants
surrounds me.
I listen, as the trees,
who are much older
and wiser than I, speak.

Leaning down
from their lofty height,
they whisper,

"We have grown tall
because we do not mind
who is the tallest
or greatest among us.
It is enough to grow together."

There is a holiness in such silence.

Years

As my years grow older
my voice grows bolder.
I devour life voraciously,
all the broken and scattered
pieces of my story;
I wonder more
and open the door
to questions
born from years of living
with both hope and fear;
If only I could see into the darkness;
would there be something more -
or someone
waiting on
the other shore?

Like a Sparrow

Fragile, like a sparrow learning to fly,
I watch my mother breathe and sigh.
"How long," I wonder,
will this breath last?
Is this the one
that will take her past?"
Breathe easy, Mom;
fly through, fly through;
if His eye
is on the sparrow,
then He's surely watching you.

There's a beauty
that comes at the end,
when there's little time to spend.
A tender smile, a faraway gaze,
curled-up fingers, simple praise.
When the light is fading,
dawn is waiting.

Finding My Way

Finding my way
through life,
I reach for something
or Someone
who might offer
safe haven;
still as I search
the skies
I find so many
black holes.

I wonder
if the end
is coming
or if I just cannot
see through
the fog

but then
a rainbow.

Home

The old house stands proudly
with a slight lean toward the garden,
gingerbread trim above the verandah.
It's not mine any more,
although I have been invited in.
The curved bannister still shines,
smelling pungent with layers of polish
and years of children sliding
gleefully to the bottom.

As I climb upward, the old fears rise with me,
the under-bed monster and that ghostly shape
in the verandah room window.
But then, around the third turn, I find
my beloved hobbit door, still there
and inviting me into my old Narnia
where I met a great lion king
and four fearless children
who taught me courage.
I enter with reverence.

Downstairs, the kitchen smells
of baked bread and blueberry pie.
I can see Mother kneading
as she waits for us to come in from chores.
We listen to the Farm Broadcast
as we eat our dinner meal.
There is static from the radio,
chatter and laughter and tears.
Outside, the potato patch holds traces
of fingers digging deep into the damp soil
building bridges and roads for our toys.

The barn also has a lean look
and the remnants in the hayloft
are sweet and crackly under my feet.
This is where I learned to crawl without fear
through tunnels of loose hay
until dinner and the night train
called me home
So much more could be written
about those childhood days

but I have life to live, much more.

Fear

Fear has been creeping in
on leaden legs
and sitting sullenly
at the back door:
we are not comfortable
with this
brooding blackness
as primordial
instincts rise;
we wander wordlessly,
seeking solace
in bright baubles
and babel talk.

But
in the distance
I hear singing;
the Lion King
is on the move
and the darkness
shall yield
to the
Light.

Janet Fisher

Ode to a Turtle Dove

So gentle and yet full of grace
you flew upon my roof.
I watch and feel
the advent
of warmer weather.

Every small thing
in the natural world
brings me to my knees
as I consider the lilies,
as I consider the bees,
as I consider the sun,
as I consider life.

Listen

listen
to what
lighthouse
has said;
the waves
how they caress
the shore;
the wind
how it whistles;
the rocks
how they crackle

friends
how they lean in
to
listen.

Grandmother

Plump and serene with a dimpled smile
and a tidy bow in her soft white hair,
she offered me nourishment amidst the storms of life:

Stewed crabapples, brown bread,
pancakes, blueberries and maple syrup
served with ample servings of wisdom and comfort
for my adolescent heart.
I loved her fiercely with all the strings of my heart.
Although legally blind and with crippling arthritis,
she was an accomplished pianist.

Simply put: she was an anchor of peace
for my hungry soul.

Thirst

"I thirst", said He.
"I'm thirsty", said she.
A sip is given.
His love,
her fears;
their Last Supper
mingled with tears.
The sky lies heavy
and low.

But across the horizon
the sun is rising.

Desert

This dry desert draws
sojourners, spent souls,
as the deer longs,
as the heart longs.
This harsh beauty,
this fragile freshness
of the dew dawn desert,
of the silty sand
and the rising rock,
stands watch over
pilgrim hearts
who seek the silence
of unknowing.

But then!
This bright sky
draws spirit upward
and a new day dawns
over a pilgrim's rest.

Cathedral Grove

My Cathedral Grove
with Her giant trees
and needled ground
and light filtering through
Her high arched dome
offered sanctuary,
a hidden place
to turn off noise
and turn on quiet,
the kind that breathes
with the night air
and the rustling leaves.

She was a host
for a little girl
seeking to be free
amidst tree majesty
and a place to wander
wordlessly
until Twilight
dropped down
Her long blue gown
to call me back
to my family.

Janet Fisher

The Sky

The sky lies low
and gray this morning,
pregnant with rain
and ready to deliver.

I am an Earth child
aching with weather pain.

Perhaps she will birth
a rainbow.
That would be
an unexpected delivery.

And a benediction.

Witnessed

I have witnessed:

A fiery, feisty firmament,
a softly spoken sentiment,
a luminous, laughing smile,
a glowing emerald isle.

And also on my way:

A newborn baby's face,
a long awaited grace,
an eagle gliding high,
a dying friend's goodbye.

And then in passing by:

A yellow rose in bloom,
a blissful bride and groom,
a broken soul in prayer,
the misty morning air.

These graces gentle me,
open my eyes to see;
my pilgrim heart then sings,
for these are sacred things.

Pandemic Recovery

The air
I breathe
a tonic;
every breath
replete;
every halting
step
a triumph;
every drop
of water
Elysian;
every breeze
on skin
a caress;
every morsel
tasted
Manna.

Life
can be so
rare.

Shadows

It takes a shadow
to bring new sight.
A lengthening darkness,
a fading of light,
turns the eye inward
and deepens the night.

I cannot say
I like the shadow
where the living is slow
and dreams fade away.
But I have learned
much from darkness.

So this I can say:
that more is found than lost,
when shadows come my way.

Memories We Keep

The memories we keep
have a varying hue,
some rosy coloured,
others dark and blue.

Laughter around a warm campfire,
the lilting sound of a children's choir.
An empty chair at a family night,
when shadows block out all the light.

Hope growing stronger every day,
friends who help along the way,
family ties reaching far and wide.
The eternal sound of a rising tide.

The memories we keep.

Homecoming

Imprisoned
In a failing body and emaciated,
grey with pain,
I look upon my friend;
and my heart is also grey and worn.
We bring him Eucharist to share, with word and prayer
and hold him in our arms and hearts.
We listen to his whispered care for loved ones dear.
And we remember
the way he shared his wisdom with us,
the way he laughed with gusto,
the way he talked with hope and looked to his loved ones,
the way he told big stories
and the way he dreamed of a bright future.
The way he downed the Eucharist.

The way he began his journey
Home.

The Night Owl

I heard the night owl call to me
and hoping I could be as free,
I called to her as best I could,
while walking in a shadowed wood.

Then in a sudden flash of light
I saw her singing in the night.
I kept my distance, as one should,
while walking in a shadowed wood.

The shadows then began to dance
as if we could be friends, perchance,
or something beautiful and good,
while walking in a shadowed wood.

I write this now with sleepy sigh
now that my night is drawing nigh;
I heard my call to Elderhood
while walking in a shadowed wood.

Pulse

I placed my finger
on the pulse
of this worn and
weary Universe
and asked,
"Where does it hurt?"
and You said,
"Here and there
and everywhere."

So I gathered You
into my arms
and bathed You
in the healing warmth
of the rising sun.

Great Spirit

Great Spirit shall give you
strength to endure,
hope for tomorrow,
wings to soar.
Mountains shall ring
with Her laughter,
as angels sing in counterpart.
Then shall She lean
close to your ear
and whisper,
"Do not fear, for I am near."

And
Her words
shall resound
In your heart.

Resting

I am resting
in the tranquility
of summer;
the sun is rising
in my heart,
fiercely warming
body and soul.

Suddenly,
I am an awakened child;
tender seeds of hope
are beginning to thrive,

Thanks be to Sea and Sky
and to our Earth's
fragrant
extravagance.

Navigate

I am navigating
my way through a surging tide
as I struggle to plumb the depths
of my long, yearning
sighs.

a universal language.

My skiff plows onward
through these deep drapes of sea,
but a malevolent undertow
wants to pull me under
into the barreling waves.

Yet
a stubborn hope
is pulling me upward
towards higher ground

and with hesitant heart,
I follow.

Tranquility

There is a tranquility
in Sabbath rest,
a time to think clearly
and a time to divest
a time to wonder
and a time to quest.

A time to ponder
and a time to cry.
A time to remember
and a time to ask why.

Melancholy

On this melancholy morning,
I rose slowly from a deep sleep
only to discover
a broken piece of life,
shattered, I thought,
beyond repair.

But then
a shooting star blazed through
and I knew it was You
inviting me to come
outside to play
and begin life anew

and so I began
to live again.

Janet Fisher

The Mirror of Time

In the mirror of time,
Happiness may seem
but a reflection,
a yearning from afar
or a fleeting glimpse
of a distant star.

Yet
She resides abundantly
in the birth of a newborn,
in the laughter of trees,
in a warm, wafting breeze.

Wait for Her melodic lyrics.
Listen to Her deep dulcet voice.
Remember Her soulful classics,
giving you reason to rejoice.

Listen-
She wants to come in
and live with you.

Arbutus Tree

Arbutus tree, so dear to me,
you peel away your skin,
to reveal what lies within,
a silvery satin sheen
of green.

In Spring you give birth
to sprays of bell-flowers
from your bounteous girth
and in Autumn
red berry bowers.

What if I could shed skin too
and begin life anew,
would I be
as bountiful as you?

Arbutus tree, so dear to me.

Lone Tree

Lone tree
on windy slope by
the sea,
what have you to teach
me of life
and loss?

Bend with the storm,
cling to the earth,
endure.

Or
look to the sky.
reach up,
grow high.

Joshua Tree

Joshua tree,
with arms held high,
you bless the strangers passing by.

Blessed are those
whose wells have run dry,
the children who cannot cope or cry,
yet still sojourn on with a will and a sigh.
Blessed are those who question "Why",
whose hearts are torn and need to mend,
who do not know what will be the end.

Blessed are you,
Joshua tree;
you urge us onward
as pilgrims free
to wander the desert
until we see.

Sunflower

She turns her face,
wearing curiosity
and blind beauty;
upwards she bends
searching for an eternal light
shining without and within;
and in the searching
is a finding;
her own auroral
brightness burning

then
she smiles.

A Summer Morning

On this glad morning
I watched a sunrise smile;
I heard the sounds
of carefree children calling;
or perhaps
it was a boisterous brook
tumbling over silver stones
or perhaps
the trees were chuckling
about the nature of things;
or perhaps
the festive flowers
were smiling secretly;
at any rate,
it was a soft serenity.

Serendipity
amidst the laughter
of a summer day.

Lullaby

As a child to her mother,
as a baby's first cry,
as a son to his father.

As a dying man's sigh.

As a lark to the blue sky,
as a bear to its den,
as an eagle that soars high.

As a deer to its fen.

As a turtle dove's soft "coo",
as the voice of a friend,
as an owl who calls "who".

As brave men defend.

Let's sing them a love song.
Enfold them in care.
And help them grow strong.

Wee Folk

The wee folk have been here,
dancing around,
gathering treasure
from the ground,
crossing the bridge
to faerie land
and singing their songs
so bonnie and grand.

And now they are seeking
to settle down
in a magical forest town
knowing their harvest
will certainly fill
their baskets with food
from the forest and mill.

Can you see them now
when you're quiet and still?

Tiger Lily

Tiger Lily,
blooming fair
in the rarest
mountain air,
you have
another name,
I think,
Chalice Cup,
a Highland drink.
Do I dare to
sip from you,
just a drop of
holy dew?

And would
your cup
be bitter

or
sweet?

Rain on Glass

As raindrops fall,
drumming downward
on the window glass,
ringing ripples on the pond,
bending the bonsai earthward,
so rain upon my heart,
Great Spirit.
Soften the heavy hardness
that lingers there
and tenderize my turmoil
with your tears.

If tears could water my soul,
it would overflow.
If my heart could speak,
it would talk of the mystery
of pain and love
and loss.

Be still, my soul and know.
Your tears are sufficient;
let them flow.

The Gardener

He tends roses,
adorns their clothes,
nurtures them tenderly,
waters them carefully.

A gentle gardener

He tends family,
encourages them wisely,
watches them grow
through joys and sorrow.

A gentle gardener

He tends friendships,
offers gentle tips,
listens from the heart,
a voice in counterpart.

A gentle gardener

On Growing Older

I carry my years within,
wisdom wrinkles written
and etched upon my skin,
the night growing colder,
a chill over the shoulder.

I greet this lurking stranger,
this stealthy, lifeline changer
with a nod and a sigh.

Someday, I am sure
I will travel to that shore
but I am not yet ready
to open the door.

A Gentle Man

He was a gentle man,
seventeen years of age
and without a game plan.
No worries and no rage.

Then the war woke the world.
He volunteered his life
as the flags were unfurled.
And so began the strife.

And when he arrived home
he was somber and still
under Earth's darkened dome.
And the air held a chill.

An inner war was raging
in his core.

Trapped

Trapped
pulled under
rogue waves
rolling me
into

an oceanic
whirlpool.

I am gasping
for air
twisted
into
a question
mark.

I cry out
but there
is no
reprieve
except for
a bitter taste
of salt

and fear.

Watching

I am watching Tree
as She extends Her arms
in dance.
She spins around singing
and gazing fondly
at Her friends, the birds;
cheerfully they sing
in unison to the sun;
this is a tender sight-
far too lovely for me
to understand fully

so I listen
and respond
in delight.

My Years

My years are etched upon my skin,
although my time seems not yet here.
Yet wiser words from wiser kin
have said that ends are always near.

Sometimes I'm lost sometimes I'm found
while traveling this rugged land.
But I am surely homeward bound
with hope clasped firmly in my hand.

I know not when my end will come
or why or how or where I'll be.
But I can hear a distant drum
calling me to a far off sea.

Sunshine and Water

When sunshine and water
call me to escape,
I become Earth's daughter
and run to undrape
Her wonders anew.

She's a beauty
to behold,
freshly dressed
in green and blue

and edged with gold.

www.ingramcontent.com/pod-product-compliance
Lightning Source LLC
LaVergne TN
LVHW011730060526
838200LV00051B/3106